100 Sewing Tips Too Good To Miss

by B. A. Anderson

First Printing: 2016

Published by B. A. Anderson

DEDICATION

In loving memory of my brother,
Anthony Anderson, Jr.
Braveheart

PREFACE

Being from a big family, the majority of our clothing came from either hand me downs or from the second hand store or friends of the family. I have been sewing, on a toy sewing machine, since the age of 6. At the age of 10, my mother bought me an adult machine. I took those hand me downs garments apart, alternating them to fit me and tailoring them for the latest fashions of the day. In my twenties, I started doing alteration and making clothing for other people. In my 40ties, I opened up a design boutique; this was before our clothing was manufactured in china. This book will tell you how to sew more in less time. If you are not organized and or focus, when you start a sewing project, it can become overwhelming to say the least. I am sharing these sewing tips that have help me throughout my 50 years of sewing and I am sure will help you too.

B. Aun Anderson

ACKNOWLEDGMENT

I would like to thank my children; Tyrone Anderson, DeAndrea Armstead, and Aaron Armstead for their ongoing encouragement and support, my parents Anthony, Sr. and Katie Anderson for their love and support. Sr.

CONTENTS

100 Sewing Tips Too Good To Miss

1. Find space for permanent sewing area.
2. List things to do for planned sewing projects.
3. Schedule sewing time like any other appointment.
4. Set realistic deadlines.
5. Organize sewing equipment, so it's permanently set up and ready to use.
6. Purchase all sewing supplies before you start.
7. Shop for several project in one trip.

8. Buy a couple of different pair of scissors.
9. Buy magnetic pin cushions and in quantities.
10. Buy tape measures in quantities.
11. Pre-shrink fabric immediately after returning from shopping.
12. Layout, cut, and marks as a group.
13. Group items that require the same thread color, so you can sew without stopping to rewind bobbins.
14. Delegate difficult sewing to a dressmaker.
15. Try team sewing.

16. Work with others in an assembly line when you must make a quantity of items.
17. Fold fabrics over hanger.
18. Store knits on a shelf or in a clear bin.
19. Store patterns in plastic envelopes.
20. Organize pattern envelopes in a portable file box.
21. Concentrate on sewing garments that can be simply constructed.
22. Put thread, pattering, notions, and supplies for project in plastic bag.

23. Group notions such as buttons, tapes, and zipper; store them in transparent boxes or jars or into a chest with clear plastic drawers.
24. Install wall-hung storage units.
25. Use an office chair that has casters.
26. Adjust chair to your height, for good back support.
27. Lower your ironing board, so you can press while seated.
28. Time saving patterns can be skill related, time related, or both.
29. *Overlock* patterns are also time savers.

30. Look at the number of pattern pieces.
31. Use less pattern pieces.
32. The more pattern pieces, the more time it takes to layout, cut and sew.
33. Analyze the details of the pattern before sewing.
34. Patch pockets are easy to sew vs. welt pockets.
35. Shaped inserts take more time.
36. Area's that call for "ease" take more time.
37. Simple seams are time saving and easy to perform.

38. Straps or belts could take an entire sewing session.
39. Remember straps or belts must be stitched.
40. Straps or belts must be turn right-side out, before sewing.
41. Using a familiar pattern pays off, by saving you fitting issues.
42. Select fabrics that are easy to work.
43. Avoid fabrics that require extensive preparation.
44. Avoid fabrics that complicate the layout.
45. Avoid fabrics that require special handling.

46. Avoid fabrics that will require extra finishing in construction steps.
47. New tools and notions are constantly being developed to help streamlined sewing.
48. Check store displays periodically, to keep abreast of what is available.
49. Keep on hand a supply of often use notions and other basic items.
50. Watch/look for sales on supplies at bargain prices.
51. For serger, keep comb thread in basic colors.
52. Use fusible interfaces to save time.

53. As you collect basic supplies, stock up on replacement parts such as *overlock* knives and machine needles.
54. Avoid discount thread.
55. Pay a little more for name brand quality thread.
56. Good quality thread looks smooth.
57. Good quality thread resists breaking.
58. Good quality thread is uniform in color, diameter, and twist.
59. Inferior (bargain basement) thread; can cause stitching problems.
60. Inferior thread can result in a garment to come apart at the seams.

61. Practice pin less sewing.
62. Save time during pattern layout, by using fewer pins or eliminating pins entirety.
63. Use a rotary cutter (instead of shears) for speed.
64. Adhesives, fusible, machine speed basting, and dissolvable basting thread are fast alternative to hand sewing or pins.
65. Use basting tape to position trims.
66. Use basting tape for appliques.
67. Use basting tape to hold zippers.
68. Use basting tape to position pockets applet.

69. Use water- suitable tape, it dissolves in first washing.
70. Use magnetic pin cushion, not only holds steel pins and needles, but for cleanup to catch stray pins and needles.
71. Reduce time spent pressing by using up-to-date pressing equipment.
72. Keep your iron in good condition.
73. Use an iron with a push button steam feature, to concentrate extra moisture where and when it is needed.

74. Fill an empty, clean roll-on deodorant bottle with water and used it to remove washable marker on right side of garment.
75. Stock up on dozens of fusible interfacings.
76. Explore the capabilities of your sewing machine.
77. Read the sewing manual.
78. Learn to use the built in stitches, attachments, and accessory box.
79. Using the same pattern pieces to cut more than one fabric, then stack them evenly, now cut both or all at once.

80. To cut layout time, either further; use push pins or weights to hold the pattern and fabric on the cutting surface.
81. Use more than one marking method within a garment, if appropriate.
82. Borrow industrial techniques, finish raw edges on an *overlock* machine, either before or after sewing seams.
83. Wipe the wheel or blades with rubbing alcohol, to remove lint and residue

84. If you use synthetic fibers, wipe the wheel or blade often during construction.

85. Use the longest stitch appropriate to the fabric.

86. Lineup garments sections, to continue sewing from one piece to another, without cutting the thread between pieces.

87. To keep seams "an even width", while sewing, watch the edge of the presser foot or the edge of the fabrics, not the needle.

88. Shorten stitch length at beginning and end of the seams, instead of backstitching.
89. Cut minutes from your sewing time by applying collars with an *overlock* machine.
90. It's easier to modify pockets on a pattern to make them faster to sew.
91. Square the corners of curve patch pockets, to save time.
92. Self-line pockets with lightweight fabric, to save sewing time.
93. Use narrow hemming foot, which automatically scrolls fabric into double fold.

94. Finish raw edges by pinkering or zigzag -stitching, before hemming.
95. Use the '*overlock* stitch' before sewing, if you are underlining a garment section.
96. Use precut strips of fusible web for fast convenient hems.
97. To sew perfectly straight topstitching on fabric without marking it, put masking tape along the fabric to establish a topstitching guide to follow. Just stitch along the edge of the tape, then remove the tape when you are finished.

98. Children's garments, have shorter seams throughout, are good for practice projects.
99. Measure twice and cut once, or be ready to head back to the store for more fabric, if it's still in stock.
100. Smile and Have Fun!

Glossary of Sewing Terms

Anchoring stitches- Machine stitches sewn with zero stitch length to keep from pulling out, or the end of seam when you stitch backwards for a few stitches to anchor the stitch.

Apex- Highest point on a rounded bulge.

Appliqué- A surface embellishment made by cutting fabric or lace designs and stitching them to the foundation fabric.

Appliqué scissors- Also known as duckbill scissors, one blade is wide for safe trimming around edges.

Armscye- Sewing term used to define the armhole.

Asymmetrical bias garment- A bias cut garment that is not a mirror image of itself from side to side.

Back tack- The end of seam when you stitch backwards for a few stitches to anchor the stitch.

Backstitch- Strong stitch that doubles back on the last stitch-perfect for securing seams and

Baste- Temporary long running stitches created by hand or machine to hold fabric in place before the final stitching.

Basting needle- A sharp, long hand sewing needle

Basting stitches- Temporary, long running stitches created by hand or machine to hold fabric in place before the final stitching.

Batiste- A fine woven cotton fabric.

Bead elastic- A strong, stretchable cord often used in beading or jewelry making.

Beeswax- A wax made by bees and used to strengthen thread for hand sewing.

Bias- True bias is a cut made on an angle 45 degrees to the selvage. This direction allows for the most stretch. Bias refers to any line diagonal to the crosswise and lengthwise grains. Most bias pattern pieces are laid on the true bias; the grainline arrow and the pattern's layout instructions will help you align your pattern pieces.

Bias binding- Also called bias tape, a bias cut strip used to bind or cover edges. Slightly stretchy, it sews neatly around curves. Can be purchased ready-made or cut from fabric.

Bias draping- Hanging bias cut fabric over a dress form to design a garment and make a pattern.

Bias seams- Seams cut and sewn on the bias.

Bias tape- Ribbons of fabric cut 45 degrees to the straight grain. Can be purchased ready-cut with folds pressed in.

Bias-bound- Bias strips of fabric used to cover a seam edge or enclose raw edges.

Bicep circumference- The measurement around the fullest part of the arm

Binding- Strip of fabric used to cover a seam edge or enclose raw edges.

Blanket stitch- Hand Stitch used for finishing a fabric edge. A smaller version is a buttonhole stitch.

Blind-hem- A hem where the stitches do not show.

Block- A master pattern.

Bodice- Upper-body portion of a garment that runs from shoulders to waist.

Bodkin- Long, flat, needle-like tool used to thread elastic through casing.

Boning- Narrow strips used to stiffen a garment, usually made of plastic, metal, or bone.

Box pleat- The two pleats face each other on one side and away from each other on the opposite side, unlike accordion pleats which all face the same direction.

Buckram- A heavy, coarse cotton fabric used for stiffening garments and hats.

Casing- Folded and stitched tunnel of fabric that holds elastic, cording, or boning.

Catchstitch- A hemstitch used to join an edge to the inside of a garment. It is formed with cross-shaped stitches on either side of an edge.

Chain stitch- A stitch formed by making connected loops that form a chain.

Chalk-trace- Pin through pattern markings, remove pattern leaving pins in place, and chalk mark the fabric using pins as a guide.

Clean finish- Term used to describe the way a raw edge is finished.

Collar stand- A band between the shirt and the collar on a shirt or blouse.

Compass rule- Any means of making a radius to form a circle such as a pin on one end of a string and a marking device on the other.

Constant reference point- A point that never changes.

Couching- Hand- or machine-sewn stitches that invisibly overcast a thread, yarn, or trim to attach it to fabric.

Couture- Highest-priced clothes from designer collections, characterized by custom fitting and hand sewing.

Crewel yarn- A two-ply, loosely twisted, fine-worsted yarn used in heavy embroidery

Crochet- A method of making a garment, fabric, braid, or lace with yarn and a hooked needle

Cross grain edge- The edge perpendicular to the selvage.

Cut-on facing- A facing extending from and attached to the same piece of fabric it's facing.

Darning foot- A presser foot with a circular opening that doesn't clamp down over the fabric and is used with dropped feed dogs for free-motion stitching or mending

Dart(s) - Folded and stitched wedges of fabric that shape a garment over curves. A dart point is marked by a dot. Dart legs are lines that come to a stop at the pattern edge.

Dolman sleeve- A sleeve style where the sleeve is cut in one piece with the bodice.

Double needle- Two machine needles attached to a single shaft. That sews two parallel rows of stitches at once with two spools of thread and one bobbin. Sometimes called a twin needle.

Double-fold hem- A hem that's folded once for the hem allowance and a second time to enclose the raw edge.

Double-layer layout- A pattern layout intended for two layers of fabric, usually including a fold for cutting half pattern pieces.

Drape- The fluid way a fabric hangs in a garment.

Ease- 1. n. Difference between body measurements and garment measurements.

Also defined as the amount of space in a garment that allows comfortable movement. 2. To slightly gather a longer piece of fabric so it can be joined to a shorter one.

Edgestitch- Straight stitching very close to the edge of a seam, trim, or outer edge. It secures seam allowances, prevents the edge from stretching, and supports the fabric.

Faced waist- A waistline finish without a band.

Facing- Used to finish exposed edges as a partial lining for center front, neckline, or armhole edges.

Facing width- The width of the facing.

Fade-out pen- A fabric pen with ink that disappears 12 to 24 hours after marking

Fashion fabric- The main fabric used to make the garment.

Featherstitch- Hand stitch used to smoothly join two layers of fabric-usually not always a seam. Also a decorative hand stitch.

Feed dog(s) - Located beneath the presser foot, these "teeth" help move the fabric under the

presser foot. In the raised position, they "feed" the fabric. You can drop the feed dogs to move the fabric freely in any direction by hand without feed dog involvement.

Fell stitch- Stitches works from the right side to pull a seam together invisibly. Stitches travel in fold fabric.

Finger press- A method of temporarily flattening a seam using the heat from your fingers.

Flat-felled seam- A seam where all raw edges are encased by fabric and sewn flat.

Float-stitch- Loosely tack fabric with stitches that are not pulled tight.

Free-motion embroidery- Hand-guided stitching with dropped feed dogs on hooped fabric.

French curve- A drafting tool that enables you to draw smooth curves.

French darts- Darts positioned on the garment front starting from near or at the waist and ending near the bust point.

French seam- A finished seam in which the seam allowance is incased by the seam.

Fusible- Fabric that has heat-sensitive adhesive on one side that enables it to bind to another fabric.

Fusible basting tape- A temporary adhesive tape that permanently fuses.

Fusible interfacing tape- Available in a variety of narrow widths, this tape heat fuses to fabric to stabilize a seam or edge.

Garment quadrant- Most single pattern pieces go 1/4 of the way around the body, such as a front bodice.

Godet- A triangular fabric piece set into a skirt hem to add fullness.

Gore- Vertical garment sections, usually on a skirt.

Gore seams- Seams that hold gores together.

Grading- The process of converting a pattern from one size to another

Grain- The orientation of the threads in woven fabric: lengthwise and crosswise. The lengthwise grain is parallel to the selvage and is the warp; cross-grain threads cross the grain and are perpendicular to the selvage.

Grainline- The long arrow symbol printed on a pattern that corresponds to the fabric grainline. It is always placed along the lengthwise grain.

Grosgrain ribbon- Characterized by woven ridges, grosgrain ribbon is very stable and comes in many widths.

Ham- A hard, stuffed form used to shape darts and curves during pressing.

Hand- The way a fabric feels in the hand, e.g. smooth, soft, or crisp.

Hand-overcast- A that wraps around an edge like a spiral.

Hem- Finished bottom edge of a garment

Hem allowance- Hem allowance is the distance between the cutting line and the hemline. This allowance is folded inside the garment before it is sewn. Also called "hem depth," it varies with the garment style and sewing technique.

Hemline- Hemline is the lowest edge of the garment once the hem is sewn.

Hip curve- A curved ruler.

Hong Kong finish- a bias-bound edge seam finish.

Hook and **loop tape**- a two part fastening device that can be sewn or glued in place.

Hoop- A plastic, metal, or wooden hoop that holds fabric tight while sewing or embroidering

Horsehair braid- A netlike ribbon woven on the bias with synthetic threads. It is stretchy and takes curves easily. Often used to add support to a hem.

Inseam- The vertical seams on pants between the legs.

Interfacing- Sew-in or fusible fabric used to stabilize the fashion fabrics. Can also add body, reinforce, or shape.

Invisible stitch- Made at 1/16-inch or 1/8-inch intervals through the side fold of the turn-under allowance. This technique hides the stitch in the fold along the edge.

Invisible zippers- A zipper designed to disappear into a seam when sewn in.

Jewel neckline- A neckline style that fits close to the base of the neck.

Jeweler's knot- A knot tied on a strand and then pulled down on a pin or needle to the base of the thread.

Ladder stitch- used to join two folded edges of fabric. Stitches are made at right angles to the fabric, creating a ladder-like formation between the fabrics, which are tightened and rendered invisible.

Lapped seams- Seams lapped one of the over the other wrong side to right side, with seamlines meeting in the center. Sewing in various ways usually a form of topstitching.

Lapel- The joining of a coat or shirt with the collar of the garment; varieties include notched and clover-leaf

Lining- Fabric (usually silky) that covers the construction details on the inside of the garment.

Longline bra- A strapless bra that extends down to the waist or below.

Lopper stitches- These are stitches formed by the looped section of a serger or overlocker.

Machine tension- Controlled by disks to apply drag to the machine thread. Adjust for thread and fabric variances.

Match point- A point marked on one pattern piece for the purpose of matching a similar point marked on a second pattern piece.

Milliner's needle- originally used by hat makers, this is a long, thin needle that does not get wider toward the eye.

Mini iron- a small iron, often with a wand-like handle, originally designed for pressing 1/4 inch quilt seam allowances.

Miter- When two strips cross at right angles the line formed by connecting the inside and outside corners.

Mitered bindings- When bindings meet at a 90 degree angle and a 45 degree seam divides them causing a diagonal seam.

Multisize pattern- A commercial pattern printed with several sizes on each pattern piece.

Muslin- 1. Unbleached cotton fabric. 2. Term used by designers to describe a test garment that checks fit and style.

Nap- A fabric texture that runs in a particular direction and requires all pattern pieces be cut facing the same direction.

Notches- Pattern marks shaped like diamonds or triangles that are printed on the cutting line of a pattern to indicate where the seams should meet.

Ombre- Closely related tones of color that graduate from light to dark

On-grain- The same as grain, straight-of-grain, or warp threads. It is a line parallel to the selvage on fabric.

Outline- The outline of a pattern is usually the cutting line, unless it is marked as a fold line.

Overcast stitch- A hand stitch that wraps around an edge like a spiral.

Pattern drafting- Drawing a paper pattern by positioning lines, points, and curves in a prescribed manner.

Peplum- An extension of a bodice below the waistline. It can be flared, pleated, cut separately from the garment, or one piece.

Pickstitch- A variation on the backstitch where you backtrack only slightly and only a bead of thread is visible on the right side of the garment

Pin-fit- Taking in seams, darts, or tucks by temporarily pinning in the seams to the right size.

Pintuck- A narrow, stitched fold of fabric. Usually seen in multiples.

Pintuck foot- A ridged foot that causes the fabric to peak up in a small tuck when sewn with a twin needle.

Piping- A narrow piece of bias-cut fabric folded over a cord and inserted into the seam between the edge and facing of a garment as a decorative trim

Pique- A textured-weave cotton

Placket- The overlapping fabric that covers an opening in a garment and supports or hides the closures. Usually a faced strip of fabric that houses either the buttons or buttonholes on a closure.

Pocket patch- Any pocket that is sewn on the face of a garment.

Point presser- A small tool used to get inside a tight corner or small space for ease of pressing

Point turner- A tool used to turn a sewn corner to the right side with a sharp, crisp point.

Preshrink- Wash fabric before cutting or sewing.

Presser foot- Holds fabric to the feed dogs on a sewing machine.

Pressing template- Shaped, heat resistant plastic, metal, or even a manila folder, used to create a smooth, crisp line or edge when pressing.

Prick stitch- Backstitch.

Princess seam- A vertical seam on blouses, dresses, jackets, or coats, usually positioned

between a side seam and the center front and back, and passing over the bust apex.

Quilt- Coverlet or wall hanging made from small pieces of fabric sewn together in batted layers and topstitched, or the action of topstitching the quilt layers together.

Raw edge- Unfinished, cut edge of fabric.

Rise- The distance between the waist band and the crotch seam on pants.

Rolled hem- The edge of fabric is rolled and stitched for a very narrow hem. Can be sewn by hand, regular sewing machine, or serger.

Rotary cutter and mat- Round cutting blade in a handle and a matt that doesn't cut.

Roving- Unspun clean fiber

Ruching- Gathering. Sometimes whole garment sections are gathered into a seam(s) or can also be ribbons of fabric gathered and used as trim.

Running stitch- Hand-sewn stitch that weaves in and out of the fabric, resulting in a dashed line.

Scallops- A series of curves or shell-like segments forming an ornamental edge

Seam- Result of two pieces of fabric stitched together. Seamline is the line that you sew along, usually 5/8 inch in from the cutting line (outermost edge of the pattern piece that you cut along). Seam allowance is the distance between the cutting line and the seamline. This allowance is usually hidden inside the garment once it is sewn. In home sewing, the measurement is conventionally 5/8 inch, but may be as small as 1/4 inch or as wide as 1 inch. Seam finish- Any technique that finishes the raw edges of a seam.

Seam roll- A cylindrical-shaped pressing tool used to press open long seams or to slide inside a sleeve for creaseless pressing.

Seam tape- A stable lightweight ribbon-like tape used to stabilize seams and finish hems.

Self-fabric- The fashion fabric.

Self-facing- Facing cut from the same fabric as the garment.

Selvage- Tightly woven factory edge of fabric that runs parallel to the lengthwise grain.

Serge- An edge or seam sewn on a serger.

Serge-finish- An edge finish sewn on a serger.

Serger- Sewing machine that can seam, trim, and overcast raw edges in one step. Also called an "overlock machine."

Set-in sleeve- A sleeve sewn into an armhole or armscye.

Shank- The back of a button through which the thread passes to attach the button to the garment.

Shoulder point- The point of the shoulder seam where the arm and shoulder connect.

Shoulder slope- The sloped angle between the side base of the neck and the point on the shoulder where the set-in sleeve begins.

Single crochet- The most basic crochet stitch.

Single-layer layout- The pattern layout for one layer of fabric. Often used for asymmetrical garments or because pattern pieces are unusual shapes or sizes.

Sizing- A starch-like fabric finish.

Slash and spread- Cutting a pattern and spreading it open along the cutline to add fullness to a section of the pattern.

Slashed pocket- A pocket cut through the face of a garment and faced.

Sleeve board- Small ironing board that fits inside a sleeve.

Sleeve cap- The area of the sleeve above the biceps line.

Slipstitch- used to join two folded edges or one folded edge to a flat surface, for an almost invisible stitch.

Sloper- Master pattern for a perfect fitting snug fitting basic garment. Used to design garments and fit commercial patterns.

Sport yarn- a particular weight of knitting yarn.

Square knot- A knot that forms a square. It's commonly used in macramé.

Stabilizer- A fabric under layer used to hold the shape of the fashion fabric or support its strength.

Staystitch- Stitching placed on or just outside the seamline, used to stabilize the fabric and keep it from stretching.

Stitch length- Length of a stitch determined by the movement of the feed dogs.

Stitch-in-the-ditch- Stitching inside the "valley" or "groove" of a seam.

Straight-grain tape- Tape cut with the grain and used to stabilize bias and cross-grain seams and edges.

Straight-stitch- The most basic machine stitch produces a single row of straight, even stitches.

Raglan sleeve- A sleeve style where the shoulder and sleeve are cut in one or two pieces.

Tambour needle- A thin, sharp pointed hook used for applying strung beads or sequins from the wrong side, or sewing decorative chain stitches from the right side.

Tapestry needle- A needle with a blunt tip and large oval-shaped eye made for decorative stitching with bulky threads or yarns

Termination point- The point where two seamlines end.

Thread chain loops- A crocheted chain made of thread and formed into a loop.

Thread tail- An untrimmed thread end.

Thread-trace- Transfer markings from your pattern to your fabric by hand basting stitches to duplicate pattern markings.

Topstitch- Decorative row of stitches sewn on the right side of a garment.

Tricot- A nylon knit fabric often used in lingerie.

Tuck- A stitched fold of fabric either decorative or used to shape a garment.

Tulle- A fine netting commonly used for veils or gowns.

Twill tape- A non-stretching tape used to stabilize seams or edges.

Underlap- The lower fabric of two overlapped pieces of fabric.

Underlay- A layer of fabric underneath another layer of fabric.

Underline- A second layer of fabric is cut from the pattern and positioned under the fashion fabric. The two layers are then sewn as one.

Underlining- a layer of lightweight fabric sewn into a garment to reinforce seams, add weight or firmness, hide construction details, and provide a layer for inner stitching.

Under stitch- When the seam allowances are stitched to the facing along an edge.

Waist stay- A stable ribbon sewn inside a dress at the waist, used to support the dress.

Walking foot- A presser foot that steps across the fabric instead of sliding to facilitate even feed.

Warp- Lengthwise thread in woven fabric that runs parallel to selvage.

Wash away stabilizer- Provides support to a fabric, then dissolves in water. It is especially useful when embroidering onto fabric.

Weft- The crosswise threads in a woven fabric--traveling from selvage to selvage.

Whiskers- Tiny, frayed threads from raw seam edges.

Wooly nylon thread- A lofty yarn-like thread that stretches to a fine straight thread when under tension. Polyester versions withstand greater heat.

Wrong side- Usually the inside of a garment or the backside of fabric.

Yardage- Term used to describe any cut length of fabric. In the U.S., fabric is measured and cut in yards (36-inch intervals). A length of fabric in an undefined amount.

Yoke- A panel either across the shoulders or at the waistline into which the bulk of the garment is sewn.

Zigzag stitch- Commonly used Z-shaped machine stitch sometimes used to finish raw edges or to sew a stretch seam.

Zipper coil- The nylon filament that spirals to form teeth in a zipper.

Zipper foot- A presser foot that enables sewing with the needle on either side--perfect for sewing close to zipper teeth.

Zipper guard- A double layer of fabric sewn behind zipper teeth as a barrier between the teeth and the skin.

Zipper teeth- Can be metal, plastic, or nylon coils each "tooth" contains the locking mechanism that holds the zipper together.

AUTHOR BIO

Barbara Aun Anderson lives in Detroit Michigan, a mother of three and a grandmother of five. She is a published writer and a vocational business instructor. Ms. Anderson holds a Master of Science degree in Administration from Central Michigan University and an undergrad degree in Communication Arts from the University of Detroit Mercy.

Made in United States
Orlando, FL
07 November 2026

90337516R00060